Travel
SOLO
to Japan

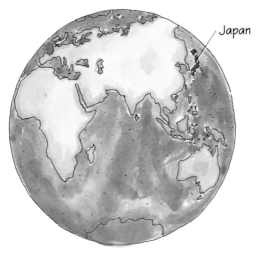

Japan

Written and illustrated
by Beth Pinkeridge

Southwood Books Limited
4 Southwood Lawn Road
London N6 5SF

First published in Australia by Omnibus Books 1999
This edition published in the UK under licence from
Omnibus Books by
Southwood Books Limited, 2001.

This edition produced for The Book People Ltd.,
Hall Wood Avenue, Haydock, St Helens WA11 9UL

Cover design by Lyn Mitchell
Typeset by Clinton Ellicott, Adelaide
Printed in Singapore

ISBN 1 903207 37 1

JAPAN

The capital
is Tokyo.

The money
is the yen.

125 million
people live
in Japan.

The language
is Japanese.

The Japanese
flag.

SEA OF JAPAN

OKI ISLANDS

KYOTO

HIROSHIMA

KYUSHU

NAGASAKI

GOTO ISLANDS

SHIKOKU

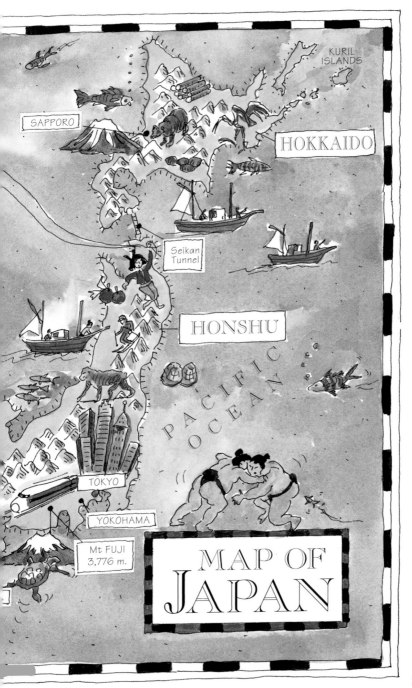

KURIL
ISLANDS

SAPPORO

HOKKAIDO

Seikan
Tunnel

HONSHU

PACIFIC
OCEAN

TOKYO

YOKOHAMA

Mt FUJI
3,776 m.

MAP OF JAPAN

3

Japan is a country of many islands.
There are four big islands and
thousands of small ones.

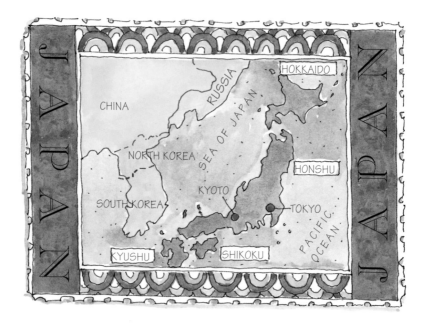

On one side, the Sea of Japan
separates Japan from China, North
and South Korea, and Russia. On the
other side is the Pacific Ocean.

Tokyo, the capital of Japan, is a very big, modern city on the island of Honshu. In Tokyo, most people live in tiny, modern flats.

Not very far away from Tokyo is the old capital of Japan, Kyoto.

In Kyoto, some people live in wooden houses that were built long ago.

The old and the new can be seen everywhere in Japan.

Japanese people take off
their shoes when they go
inside their houses. They
put on plastic slippers.

In an old Japanese house
there are *tatami* mats on
the floor. These are made
from rice straw.

In these older houses, instead of walls there are sliding doors made from wood and rice paper. In summer, these doors can be taken off. This makes the house one big, airy room.

It is polite to take a bath before dinner, but many Japanese homes have no bath tub.

People pay to go to a public bath house, or *sento*. An attendant gives out a towel, soap, a wash bowl and a cloth.

Everyone must be clean before getting into the hot bath.

Men and women bathe separately.

The *kimono* is a beautiful robe made from silk or cotton. Once all Japanese people wore the *kimono*. Now it is usually worn only for festivals or the tea ceremony, or when visiting shrines.

Some people wear a *kimono* every day as their uniform. Wooden clogs called *geta* are worn with the *kimono*.

Most people in Japan wear modern clothes.

Japanese people like to eat rice and noodles and fish. Table manners are very important, but young children can eat with their fingers.

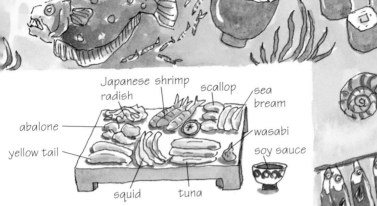

Japanese shrimp
radish
scallop
sea bream
abalone
wasabi
yellow tail
soy sauce
squid
tuna

Sashimi is raw fish. It is eaten with rice and *wasabi*, a hot sauce like mustard.

Millions of pairs of chopsticks are used every day in Japanese restaurants. They are used once and then thrown away.

KYUSHU SHIKOKU HONSHU HOKKAIDO

The islands of Japan are really the tops of mountains. Millions of years ago movements of the earth pushed the mountains out of the sea.

Violent movements still cause earthquakes and volcanic eruptions.

The most famous volcano is Mount Fuji, the highest mountain in Japan.

When the earth moves under the ocean, it can create a giant wave called a *tsunami*.

The *tsunami* begins as a long, low wave. It travels very quickly across the ocean, but slows down as it comes to shallow water. When it reaches the coast it is sucked back into the sea, just like an ordinary wave, but this wave becomes bigger and bigger.

The giant wave crashes over the land and causes terrible damage.

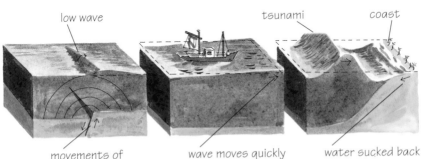

low wave

tsunami

coast

movements of the earth on the ocean floor

wave moves quickly

water sucked back

There are many ways to travel around Japan. The bullet train, or *shinkansen*, is a super-fast train that can go at 270 kilometres an hour. There are earthquake detectors built into the electric track. If there is an earthquake, the system shuts off.

An old story tells how Japan was
made. A god and goddess stirred an
oily mixture with a long spear. When
this thickened they dropped some off
the spear and it formed an island. The
god and goddess married and had
children, who became the main islands
of Japan.

There are many myths about strange spirits that live in trees, rivers and in the sea. Some spirits are good, but some are very scary.

A *kappa* is a bad water spirit. It is supposed to trick people and animals so that they drown.

kappa

In Japanese myths, the fox looks after the rice crop and is very fierce.

At Mount Inari there is a shrine to the god of rice with many statues of foxes.

Brown bears, monkeys, cranes and badgers are some of the animals found in Japan. The snow monkey and the Japanese giant salamander are found nowhere else in the world.

Snow monkeys

The Japanese giant salamander

There used to be many whales in the sea off Japan. Japanese fishermen hunted whales for their meat, and now there are very few. A world ban on killing whales has not stopped this hunting.

MONKEY

3.00

7.00

HERON

3.00

OCTOPUS

8.00

SNAKE

6

OWL

3.00

SQUID

WHALE

10.00

TUNA

10.00

DOLPHIN

10.00

The Japanese have a special respect for natural materials such as wood, straw, earth, paper and bamboo.

In the past everything was made from these, but today many things are made from plastic.

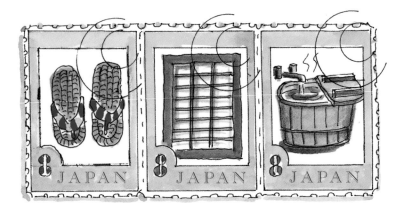

Some things are used once and then thrown away. Even old bikes that are still good are thrown away. Old cars are kept off the roads to keep pollution down. People are encouraged to buy new cars.

The main religions in Japan are
Shintoism and Buddhism. Shinto means
"way of the gods". It teaches that
there are millions of gods called *kami*.
They live in sacred places such as
rivers, mountains and trees.

A gateway or *torii* marks the entrance
to a Shinto shrine.

4 A torii.

50 A Shinto shrine.

5 Paper blessings for good fortune.

8 Shinto priests.

1 Ropes mark sacred ground.

20 Visitors must wash their hands and mouth before they enter a temple.

27

Buddhism started 2,500 years ago, in India. The Buddha was a wise and kind teacher who taught people how to be happy.

Buddhists believe that after people die, they can be born again as an animal or as a human.

Buddhist monks shave their heads and wear simple robes. They have no money of their own. Buddhists worship at a simple shrine. They make offerings of flowers, candles and incense.

Education is very important in Japan. Children must study hard and get good marks. If they do not, they may not get a good job.

If Japanese children are sick, their mothers can go to school for them. They take notes in class to make sure their child will not fall behind.

School starts at 8.30 in the morning and finishes at 4.30 in the afternoon. There is even school on Saturdays. Older children often go back to school at night for extra study.

Children in Japan must help clean their school every day during the lunch break.

木 手 休 土

足

分

自

金 国 体 大

Japanese is written in three different ways. One way of writing is called *kanji*. *Kanji* is made up of many different characters. A character is writing that comes from a picture, like this.

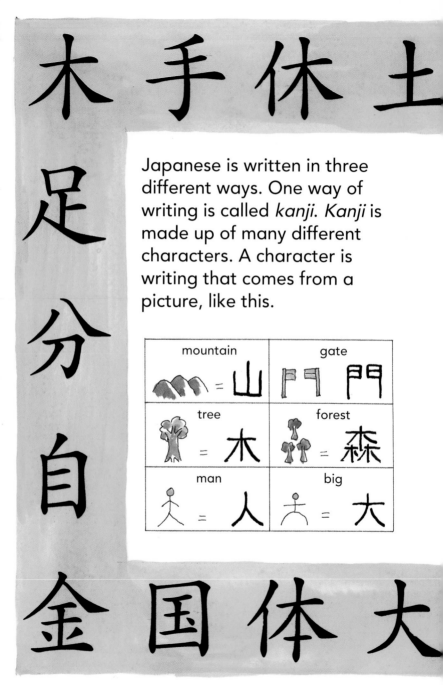

mountain	gate
tree	forest
man	big

畑 身 本 見

時

刀

林

page turns
this way

start
here

9

8

Japanese people start writing
from the top right-hand corner
of the page and write
downwards. They read from
right to left.

筆 竹 雨 森

brush

ink   water

Calligraphy is the art of beautiful
handwriting. Japanese children study
this at school. They paint letters on
paper using a brush and special black
ink. It looks easy, but it is hard to learn.

The Japanese have been making paper for a very long time.

They make it from plants such as *kozo* (paper mulberry) and *mitsumata*.

This handmade paper, called *washi*, is used to make dolls, masks, kites

... paper screens, lanterns and toys.

In the past, life for children in Japan
was very strict. Grandparents lived at
home with the family. Children had to
learn to write, dance, and play music.
They had to be very polite to their
elders. It is still important in Japan to
respect old people.

Many families now have only one child,
and so these children are sometimes
very spoilt.

Bowing is an important part of everyday life in Japan. Instead of shaking hands, the Japanese bow.

JAPAN

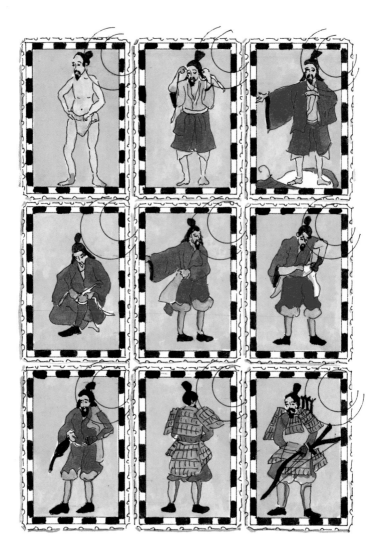

Hundreds of years ago, noble warriors called *samurai* lived in Japan. A *samurai* took a long time to get ready for battle.

Samurai would rather die than be captured by the enemy. A *samurai* would kill himself by putting part of his sword into his stomach. Then his servant would chop off the *samurai*'s head. This was called *seppuku*.

Judo and *kendo* are martial arts. They began as *samurai* fighting skills. In *kendo*, students learn to fight with long sticks.

Many children learn *kendo*. They dress up like *samurai*, with a face mask, breast plate and gloves. They fight with wooden swords.

There are no weapons used in *judo*.
The word *judo* means "gentle way".

In a *judo* school, the colour of the belt
tells what level a student has reached.
Beginners start with a red belt, then
after a test, move on to white. The
next belts are yellow, orange, green,
blue, brown, and finally black.

eri (collar)

obi (belt)

Long ago there were many castles
in Japan. Warlords built them
in high, rocky places
to keep out
their enemies.

A castle was built out over the walls so that stones could be dropped on the enemy if they climbed up.

Peepholes in towers made it easier to see the enemy, and to aim at him.

A fish-shaped dragon on the castle roof was a good luck charm against fire.

Making and drinking green tea has been a special art in Japan for many years.

The tea is made in a beautiful teapot, and stirred using a hand-made whisk.

Then it must be drunk in exactly three-and-a-half sips.

All of this is done in a tea house in a lovely garden.

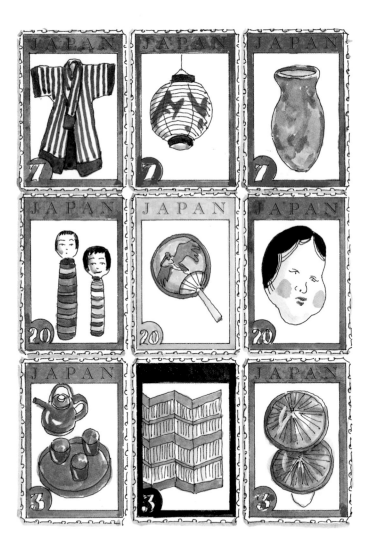

The Japanese admire beautiful things and the people who make them. The best artists and crafts people are called "Living National Treasures".

Clay, stone, wood and paper are some of the materials these artists use. They teach students their special skills.

The Japanese have their own kinds of musical instruments that make their music sound very special.

The *shamisen* has three strings. It is played in puppet theatre and in *kabuki* theatre.

The *shakuhachi* is a simple bamboo flute. To play it you blow across the end, not across holes in the side.

The *biwa* is played by hitting a plectrum strongly against the string.

The *koto* has many strings. It is played by picking the strings with small picks that are worn on the fingers.

This wooden fish is a drum used in Buddhist ceremonies in Japan. It is hit with a stick.

People of all ages love going to the theatre in Japan.

Bunraku is a puppet theatre where plays are acted by puppets to the music of a *shamisen* and the chant of a storyteller.

In *kabuki* theatre, there are only male actors. Female parts are played by men. *Noh* is a kind of dance that tells a story. All the actors wear masks.

52

Sumo wrestling is a very old sport. A *sumo* wrestling match is called a *basho*. The wrestlers try to push each other out of a small ring. They are huge men who must eat very fattening food to stay big. *Sumo* wrestlers are famous all over Japan.

There are many festivals in Japan.

Kodomo-no-hi, a children's holiday, is held in May. Families with boys fly streamers made to look like *koi*. A *koi* is a fish. It represents strength.

In November there is a festival called
Shichi-Go-San. Girls aged seven and
three and boys aged five go to shrines
and temples dressed in their best
clothes.

Setsubun is
another special
day in February.
Children dress up
in demon masks
and throw soya
beans at
each other.

In Japan there are many ways to wish for good luck. One way is to buy a lucky charm. This can be a picture or a small statue.

A *daruma* is a picture of a face. Someone making a wish paints one eye on the face. The other eye is painted on when the wish comes true.

The cat statue, or *maneki-neko*, is put up in the window of a shop to bring customers and wealth inside.

If someone is sick, Japanese people send paper cranes. The crane is a symbol of good health and a long life.

There are so many people in Japan that special "pushers" have the job of pushing passengers on to the already crowded trains.

The world's longest tunnel under the sea, the Seikan Tunnel, is in Japan. It is nearly 54 kilometres long. Trains run through it.

HOKKAIDO

tunnel

HONSHU

The worst earthquake in history happened in Japan. The shaking ground overturned stoves, setting many wooden houses on fire.

Hotels in Japan are very expensive. Many people can only afford to stay in "capsule" hotels. Each capsule is 1.2 metres by 1.2 metres by 2 metres deep. It has a bed, a television, a light, an alarm clock and a shelf.

Know?

Japanese women once used to paint their teeth black. This was because they used white make-up on their faces, which made their teeth look yellow.

The Japanese think it is very rude to blow your nose in public. You should just keep sniffing until you are somewhere by yourself.

Japan has the largest number of vending machines in the world. They sell everything from food to clothing.

The highest tidal wave on record hit Japan in 1971. It was 85 metres high – almost as high as New York's Statue of Liberty.

59

GLOSSARY

basho ★ *sumo* wrestling match.

biwa ★ musical instrument with strings.

Buddhism ★ religion that worships the Buddha.

bullet train ★ one of the fastest trains in the world.

bunraku ★ puppet theatre.

calligraphy ★ the art of writing.

geta ★ wooden clogs worn with a kimono.

judo ★ art of self-defence.

kabuki ★ theatre where men play women's roles.

kami ★ spirits that live in trees, rocks, and mountains.

kanji ★ a Japanese way of writing, with characters that come from pictures.

kappa ★ mythical creature supposed to live in rivers.

kendo ★ art of fencing using a bamboo stick.

kimono ★ traditional robe.

koto ★ musical instrument with strings.

myths ★ old stories of gods and heroes.

noh ★ a form of theatre where all actors wear masks.

samurai ★ Japanese warrior.

sashimi ★ dish made of thinly sliced raw fish.

sento ★ public bath house.

seppuku ★ the way a *samurai* killed himself.

shakuhachi ★ musical instrument like a flute.

shamisen ★ musical instrument with strings.

shinkansen ★ bullet train.

Shinto ★ religion that worships nature spirits.

sumo ★ Japanese wrestling.

tatami ★ floor mats made of straw.

tsunami ★ tidal wave.

warlords ★ leaders from long ago who took power by force.

wasabi ★ hot Japanese sauce.

washi ★ handmade paper, made from plants.

INDEX